DICKY SLADER

DICKY SLADER

THE EXMOOR PEDLAR POET

by

J. M. SLADER

Preface by A. J. Butcher
North Devon journalist and broadcaster

FORGE BOOKS
WOKINGHAM
BERKS
1995

© Copyright 1995
J. M. SLADER
First published in 1963 by David & Charles who
have kindly assented to this new edition

Printed in Great Britain by
Short Run Press Ltd, Exeter

CONTENTS

List of illustrations	7
Preface	9
A Yeoman's Son	11
Early Days at Hunnawins	16
The Pedlar of Molland Cross	23
Friends and Neighbours	32
Moorland Exploits	41
1914-1918 and Afterwards	49
Alone with his Memories	57

LIST OF ILLUSTRATIONS

Between pages 32 and 33

I. 'At home'

II. William Slader

III. Mary Ann Slader

IV. Thomas Slader

V. Betsy

VI. In his Sunday best

VII. His home

VIII. In his garden

IX. Surrounded by his poultry

X. At his cottage gate

XI. With Colonel Hall

XII. The outing to Ilfracombe

To my Wife, without whose assistance
this work would not be possible

To all those Devonians who either
knew Dicky Slader or could provide
information. Without their help this
life story would be uncompleted

PREFACE

THIS story of a man who has become part of the history of Exmoor demanded someone with his roots in the moor to write it. The author although living in Wales knows more about the Exmoor Forest and the people who lived there in the last century than any writer I know.

Dicky Slader will always be an enigma. He was never such a fool as he looked—but he was not always the gentleman he fancied himself to be. He was a man who hid a quick wit behind a simple exterior and he was far more of a 'scholar' than most of his Exmoor neighbours believed him to be.

What is most remarkable about Dicky Slader is that although he was a figure of fun and was looked upon to some extent as a kind of 'poor white' by the established farmers and gentry, he had it in him to write simple hymns of undoubted sincerity.

But above all Dicky was a 'character'—perhaps one of the last of the great Exmoor eccentrics. He left his mark upon the moor for all time, and J. M. Slader, the author of this book, has made sure that Dicky Slader will join the immortals.

A. J. Butcher

A YEOMAN'S SON

> God's precious gifts are not a few,
> They fall from heaven above
> Just like the gentle morning's dew,
> Perfumed with hallow'd love.

IN those parishes along the southern and western spurs of Exmoor it is not difficult to imagine life a century ago. This is still a remote region far from industry and the pace of modern urban life. Only a solitary jet from Chivenor on the shores of Barnstaple Bay reminds us on occasion of this uncertain 20th century in which we find ourselves.

The Sladers had farmed the bleak acres beneath the wild moor for many centuries. One of the yeoman families of old England, justly proud of their heritage, they had produced many sons. Whilst not famous they had made their mark, in the church, in the legal profession, on the sea and upon the soil.

Hunnawins lies in a fold in the rolling fields overlooked by the heights of Exmoor rising to over 1,600 feet at Five Barrows on Western Common. A comparatively modern farm in a parish of ancient settlements, the farmhouse was built just prior to the commencement of the 19th century. Surrounding it are such homesteads as Hunstone, Popham, Bornacott, Eworthy, Bentwitchen, and Stitchpool, all farmed by Sladers down through the centuries.

On 29 May 1857 Mary Ann Estcomb in the tradition of hard-working Victorian wives bore her husband William

Slader his tenth child, a son whom they christened Richard. The scene at Hunnawins on that sunny May morning was very little different from the previous nine occasions upon which another Slader had been brought forth into the household. Betsy, the first-born and already 18 years old, was the hard-working maid of all work, helping her father and mother and carrying out the same duties as just three years previously at the birth of her brother David. Between herself and David there was Mary Jane, her junior by just two years, then Elizabeth and John, Susannah, William, Michael, and Thomas.

Richard was born into a community that was still untouched by the industrial revolution already gaining momentum in the Midlands and the North, into a parish which still knew its bounds as the far-distant markets of Barnstaple and Bampton, a parish of folklore adjoining that expanse of desolation and utter wildness not surpassed for rough wild beauty in all our land.

The birth of a son in that farming community was an event of no mean importance. Daughters passed unnoticed, but sons were the lifeblood of the farmer's homestead, and as was usual news of the birth of Richard quickly spread across this extensive and lonely parish.

Richard's father was churchwarden of North Molton church and the Rev Burdett was amongst his closest friends. On that following Sunday morning as he stepped into the trap for the two-mile trot he was accompanied by his 13-year-old son John, the eldest, already taking a useful part in the day-to-day running of the farm. Young John was a bright, hard-working lad, and since leaving school the previous year, had shown great promise as another farmer in the Slader tradition. The coming of yet another brother in the name of Richard did not seem to affect his life at all and he was but vaguely aware of the main talking point that Sunday morning after church, as relations and friends alike congratulated his father. Matins at North Molton was the weekly meeting-place of lord and labourer, rich and poor. Unlike for the weekly market in nearby South Molton, everyone was dressed in Sunday best, the topic of conversation not pigs and politics but parson and parishioners.

The early years at Hunnawins in that isolated parish overlooked by the wild expanse of Exmoor were very quiet. Times were hard and farmers with their sons laboured from dawn to dusk for little return. Even the mine down in the valley at Heasley Mill had fallen upon hard times.

Once Dicky could walk he was anxious to wander and it became increasingly difficult for his mother to keep him within the bounds of the farm, let alone the house. As soon as he was old enough he was taken along to the Charity School down in North Molton. His brother Thomas was the star pupil, and Mrs Passmore, the mistress, was quick to welcome another of the Slader family. Thomas was only three years older and the two brothers became inseparable.

From his early schooldays Dicky was something of a character. He would sit and dream for hours on end, whether in the classroom or in the hayfield. Country life and people fascinated him. From an early age he was a happy child, always having an answer for whoever might stop him, and many times a humorous one. Whether it was Lord Poltimore himself or Peter Bird, the village blacksmith, Dicky was always ready. By the age of ten he had so taken his place in the parish that every cottager and farmer knew of young Dicky. At school, when Mr Cambridge took over from Mrs Passmore, he was known to saunter in just when he liked. Sometimes Sammy Cambridge would go out into the square if he saw Dicky passing and call him in. Sometimes he would 'be too busy', as he used to say, and at other times he would follow Sammy in to sit beside him at the front of the class. In his early teens Dicky used to go to Sunday School up at the small Wesleyan chapel at Molland Cross, with his brother Thomas. It was nearer than walking to the church. The tales of John Wesley and his exploits in the neighbourhood used to fascinate him and at an early age he obtained a book of his sermons. He read, too, the Bible and even in those tender years could recite the 43rd Psalm.

Whenever he could, Dicky would get away from the farm and explore. He would walk for miles on his own, down by the River Mole, up over Yard Down, even on to the heights of Exmoor itself. Many times he would be missing from home but his father and mother never worried. As a small boy he would be found speaking in his broad Devonshire brogue to the vicar in the square at North Molton, to the captain of the Bampfylde Mine, or to some of the rugged Cornish miners outside the notorious Acland Arms, at Moles Chamber. People used to say that 'young Dicky Slader from Hunnawins' was destined for greater things.

His father would often take him to market with his brother John. There he would jostle with all the farmers of the district and meet colourful characters. It was at South Molton one market day that young Dicky was introduced to Parson Joseph Jekyll of the Exmoor parish of Hawkridge. Jekyll was a contemporary of one of Dicky's cousins when at school at Blundells, and he had always listened intently at home to tales of this gentleman and his fox-hunting partner, the Rev John Russell. He pictured him as rather a cruel huntsman with no time for the yeoman farmer. Although Dicky was only 12, he carried on quite an intelligent conversation with the old parson and after a while, looking at the horse standing by, said, 'That be a fine looking 'oss you 'ave there, parson'. Jekyll, always proud of his steed and the stock from which he

A YEOMAN'S SON

was bred, exclaimed, 'The finest horse about these parts. From a gentleman's racing stables up Somerset way. Catch the fastest fox west of Dunster.' 'Really,' said Dicky, 'me varther has a girt 'oss, bred from yeoman stock, git you to Barum quicker than it takes your 'oss to catch that fox.' Poor Parson Jekyll was taken back a bit at the youngster's speech and quickly suggested he should find his father in case he should be wanting to start back home.

By the time Dicky was 15 his sister Betsy and his brother Thomas had both left home. Betsy, the eldest of the family and a second mother to Dicky, had married and gone to live in Manchester. A short while afterwards Thomas entered the Wesleyan ministry, following in the footsteps of his cousin William from Longstone Wells, a remote farm standing high on the moor above South Radworthy. Dicky expressed a wish to follow his brother into the ministry but the family finances did not allow this. He could not see this though; he felt God had overlooked him for associating with an uncouth ostler at the George. Family life on that remote farm a century ago was very close. For some time after his closest brother and sister had left home, he was always waiting for the footsteps of the postman. If he was down on the road he would sometimes beg a lift from Dr Spicer, who often passed by on his chestnut hunter. Jumping up on the horse's buttocks, he would say, 'Don't ee mind me, Doc, I be only going to see Burgess the post'. And down to the Post Office he would go. 'Have yer more letters from Thomas and Betsy?' he would enquire of Henry Burgess, the postmaster.

EARLY DAYS AT HUNNAWINS

> 'Tis God that gives those fruitful showers
>   Which make the grass to grow,
> His shining name we read on flowers,
>   And rivers as they flow.

THIS period as Dicky was growing into manhood was, in spite of the isolated existence of his later years, about the loneliest of his life. He often played truant from the farm, and his parents could never rely on him. His life, it appears, was full of dreams of what he would do. He became unsettled at home and often thought of moving away. The call of the country, however, 'his parish' and 'his chapel', were too great, and the call of the industrialised Midlands for still more labour made no impact on him.

In 1873 his brother John left home to try his luck abroad and joined the many thousands of that period who emigrated to that new land of opportunity across the broad expanse of the Atlantic. It was about this time that Dicky heard that Mr James Julieff, the captain of Bampfylde Copper Mine, was seeking a manservant. Longing to be independent of home ties he applied for the post and was taken on a week's trial. At the end of the probationary period he was back on the farm. 'Not going to work for any Baptist foreigner,' was Dicky's comment. From an early age it was evident Dicky was very independent. Julieff was a devout Baptist and this didn't go down at all well.

Another tale told of him during his late teens concerns the

EARLY DAYS AT HUNNAWINS

Rev William Stephenson, the Wesleyan superintendent minister at Barnstaple, when he preached at a special service at Molland Cross Chapel. After the service Dicky, who was with his elder brother Michael, went up to the minister and said, 'That be a right good'un you preached, Reverend, 'bout the best I've heard in this yer chapel.' 'I'm glad you think so, Richard,' answered Stephenson, who, knowing the family, was prepared for some comment from the well-dressed lad who had sat in the front pew. He had noticed that he had taken in every word of his 30-minute sermon. 'Only one trouble,' said Dicky, ''twas too long. I could have said what you said in half the time. My backside is right sore now, just as if I'd ridden an 'oss from here to Bristol.'

During this period up until he was 24 when his mother died, the visiting clergymen fascinated him, and whenever such gentlemen called and the cider was drawn from the keg, he would sit down and listen intently to the conversation. The Anglican parsons of this isolated neighbourhood during those years were real characters, the stories of whom have already passed into folklore. Several of them personally knew Froude of Knowstone during the notorious years of his 'reign'. Russell after a day's hunting up on the moor would pass by on his homeward trek to Swimbridge. How Dicky loved it when the conversation turned to this gentleman's exploits at Sandringham, how his hunting friend Prince Albert had requested the pleasure of his company, 'and tell him not to forget to bring his sermon so that the Queen will learn a little of the merits of this West Country Parson'. There were also Carwithan of Challacombe, Pyke of Parracombe, Karslake of Meshaw, Winnifrith of Mariansleigh, and Blackmore of Charles. The Rev Richard Blackmore was a frequent visitor at Hunnawins and Dicky would love to get him talking about his grandmother Elizabeth Slader. Many tales were told of the two families a century previous and he was fascinated.

Dicky would love to visit Charles Rectory and he would chat with Blackmore's wife if the rector himself wasn't at home. On a couple of occasions he met the parson's nephew, R. D. Blackmore, and it may have been his early meeting with this literary gentleman and the stories told of him by his uncle that led Dicky to have some of his own works printed. He was a great reader and Blackmore's novels, centred as they were on the pastoral scene that he loved so well, took pride of place alongside the family Bible and Wesley's Sermons.

In September 1881 Dicky's mother died, and a few days later she was laid to rest alongside the other members of her family in North Molton churchyard. All the family with the exception of John in America returned home. It was a sorrowful occasion for she had been well loved. Dicky being the youngest felt it most, and missed her terribly. Without her he felt his protection from the outside world had gone.

After this loss his father engaged a servant to help about the house. She lived at the farm and looked after David and Richard who were now the only ones at home. To them fell the increasing responsibility of farming. William Slader, Dicky's father, was now becoming frail, and only three-and-a-half years later, in March 1885, he too passed on. Again there was a family reunion. John came home from the Mid-Western States where he had built himself up a cattle ranch. For the last time the ten children of Hunnawins were together.

Many stories have circulated over the years concerning Dicky and his father's will. It is said he arranged for the family solicitor to come to the house at a time when his brothers and sisters were away at South Molton market. There is some truth in this story for Dicky himself used to relate such a tale with amusement. There is no doubt that the one he told was nearest to what actually happened.

EARLY DAYS AT HUNNAWINS

When his father was ill on one occasion a lawyer was sent for to make a will. Richard was afraid that his brother David, who had been a loyal son, might get a larger share under the will than he himself, and as David was in the house when the lawyer arrived, Richard thought also that his brother might influence his father at the crucial moment. Richard thereupon went to a field on another part of the farm and drove some sheep from where they were grazing into a field of corn; then he ran to the farmhouse and raised the alarm, thus drawing David away to drive the sheep from the cornfield.

After his father was laid to rest the family gathered around the solicitor to hear the will read as was the custom in those days. Dicky said : 'Read it again, it sounds so good'. 'Betsy £5, Mary Jane £5, Elizabeth £50, Susanna £50, John £25, if he comes and claims it, William £100, Michael £100, Thomas £25, Richard £300 and Bratton Club (approx. £50). David all the rest and sole executor. All sums payable on March 25th, 1886.' It was no wonder that Dicky said it sounded so good. He had apparently induced his father to favour him by indicating that as he was not so bright and learned as his brothers and sisters he should have a bigger share. As Thomas wrote his brother John at the time : 'The will is not a very fair one but as it cannot now be altered it is no good to say anything about it.' The rest of the family accepted the position and it did not apparently dawn upon any of them at that time that this was engineered by the not-so-bright brother who was left at home.

After this final break with the past, with his father and mother passed on, there began a period of ten years when Dicky lived at the farm with his brother David more as a labourer than a partner. David had brought his wife to Hunnawins the previous year, and only three months after his father died twin sons were born. The relationship between

Dicky and his brother had never been really amicable. The brothers were opposite in many ways, David being rather the good-time lad of the family. Their father's will did not improve this relationship, and when Dicky, after working hard from dawn to dusk, saw his brother coming home of an evening rather the worse for drink, it angered him. David had no time for his brother's chapel, and although his wife Sarah cared for Dicky, prepared his meals and darned his socks, the relationship deteriorated.

It was during these years that he would sit down in his room of an evening and write his poetry. Friends that visited the farm in those days would remark upon the quiet young man with his notebook and pencil who said so little. During the daytime he was kept so busy that he had little opportunity to wander down the lanes and up over the moor that he loved so well. Occasionally on a Wednesday he would break away into South Molton market. It was not so much the cattle that interested him as the colourful characters drawn to this market town: the travelling salesmen from Bristol and up country; the hurdy-gurdy, with its cheeky monkey, grinding out a series of monotonous and popular tunes; the jolly fool, the ancestor of the circus clown, in his cloak of many colours amusing the children; the sideshows travelling from market to market.

After the hubbub of the market-place had died down there was, at election times, the political meeting which was by no means the quiet dignified discussion of ideas which it is today. Dicky would listen intently, and when the shouting began and the air became thick with bad eggs and ripe tomatoes, he would creep away and return to the quiet of Hunnawins. A story is told of the 1892 General Election. The supporters of Mr R. A. Moore-Stevens, the Conservative candidate, sent a pony and trap to bring Dicky in to vote. He gracefully accepted the offer and after going indoors for his top hat, which was reserved for Sundays, funerals and elections, he proceeded to the polling booth in North Molton. As he told a friend later, 'I couldn't refuse the offer of riding behind those nice-looking gentlemen, but I could hardly let me friend George Lambert down. He be sure to win with the Sladers behind him.' Indeed, George Lambert, the Liberal candidate, did come top of the poll.

At Molland Cross on a Sunday something was missing if Dicky was not in his pew beneath the pulpit. Only a severe chill, and this was a rarity in the healthy surroundings of Hunnawins, would keep him away 'from his duty', as he would say. This little stone chapel, one of the cradles of nonconformist Christianity in the Exmoor border country, echoed with the sound of joyful voices twice every Sunday. Already Richard Slader was known for his allegiance to his chapel, his tenor voice and his abstinence from alcoholic liquor, 'except cider,' as he would say, 'a product of God's land.'

It was about this time that Hunnawins, one winter's night when the icy blast was blowing down from Five Barrows, was destroyed by fire. David, it is said, was occupying his usual settle down at the Poltimore Arms, and his wife and children had little time to save anything. Within a few minutes it was a blazing inferno. Dicky had just attended to the turkeys, prior to closing them up for the night. (Since he was a small boy and his mother had taught him how to rear turkeys, he looked upon this as his charge—'the birds of Christ's mass', he would say.) All he managed to save, as he told a friend years later, was 'me top hat, me Bible and me verses'.

The verses were, in fact, a collection of 50 poems which Dicky set to many of the well-known hymn tunes. There was not a tune in the Wesleyan Hymnal which he could not sing without any prompting. In this year of 1892, through the help of a family friend, he was able to get his collection published, 'printed by W. C. Coles, at his Machine Printing Works, Grenville Street, Bideford'. These songs and hymns were all dedicated to the various religious sects which were so alive in the North Devon of 70 years ago—this was at the close of that 50-year era when the nonconformists had built their chapels at every crossroads. Wesleyans, Primitive Methodists, Baptists, Plymouth Brethren, Bible Christians, Congregationalists, and Salvationists, they had all been particularly active in the parishes between Exmoor and Barnstaple Bay. Everyone went to chapel or church, so much so that the Anglicans were enlarging their churches to accommodate the increasing congregations.

Dicky's life at this stage took a complete change. Although Hunnawins was being rebuilt, the gulf between him and his brother David widened, so much so that he tended to neglect his duties on the farm, and often he would be found in the markets or wandering about the highways of this large and isolated parish. He would stop for a chat with all the farmers' wives, who began to welcome him, for there was nothing they liked more than a little gossip. If there was any news to be had, Dicky knew it. And so towards the close of the Victorian era Dicky took a little cottage near his chapel at Molland Cross, quite close to his old family homestead. He cut himself off from his family, became independent and set up house on his own. Here he was to spend the rest of his life, 30 years as a near-hermit, 'an eccentric', as he was sometimes known, 'a nut and taty trader', as he called himself.

THE PEDLAR OF MOLLAND CROSS

> Come, all mankind, rejoice and sing,
> Let praise your lips employ,
> Give thanks to God, our heavenly King,
> With love that cannot cloy.

THE fame of Richard Slader as a writer of poetry and hymns spread far and wide over the pastoral scene of North Devon and the wild expanse of Exmoor into West Somerset. The farmers occupying the lonely windswept homesteads of the Knights, those pioneers of the 19th century in this part of the country, now so strongly associated with Blackmore's *Lorna Doone*, read and sung with reverence the hymns of this country boy from their neighbouring parish. For many a long hour Dicky would sit and think in his little cottage, penning his words on paper. Alas! most have been lost to the modern world.

From the outset of his move from Hunnawins Dicky knew he had to make his own living to survive. As was the custom in the countryside of over 60 years ago nuts, particularly hazel nuts, from the hedgerows were one of the staple foods of the farmer and his family. Dicky was wide awake to the possibilities of trade in this easily-procured commodity, and many an autumn morning he would be found at Yardswell Cross, Bentwitchen, or even as far as Bratton Down with his sack slung over his shoulder, sometimes a beret resting on top of his head and the crook of the shepherd in his hand. Vaguely reminiscent of a Spanish pirate, he would salute everyone he met, neighbours and strangers alike. His sheepdog, Sammy, was always by his side, not only as companion but to show, as he would say, 'a varmer's son'. 'Au me gran'-vather an' gurt gran'-vather waz varmers avore in their time', he would tell you before many minutes had passed. To Dicky the possession of a sheepdog gave him status, in much the same way as a squire had to have his chestnut hunter.

With his 'nits' and his garden produce he set up as a pedlar and at the turn of the century he became well known at all the markets and fairs in the neighbourhood, from Lynton to Barnstaple, Combe Martin to Bampton. Often at South Molton he would be seen wearing a faded old-fashioned bowler with a high crown, and a tattered long tail-coat. His thin face with its prominent nose had the sad, almost beseeching, look of a favourite dog discarded by its master. And to add that a dewdrop inevitably glistened at the tip of Dicky's nose is important, because this was tied up with his almost perpetual habit of sniffing loudly between sentences.

Between markets Dicky would travel the dusty roads in this Exmoor border country selling his nuts, carefully dried during the winter months. He took pains to point out to dubious farmers' wives that he was very particular in his final selection. 'Tull 'ee wat' (he began nearly every sentence with this curious phrase). 'Tull 'ee wat now, Missis, you won't vind wan nit een a pound that's dreeve.' A 'dreeve' nut in Dicky's idiom was one which looked right until you cracked it. Then all you found inside was a miserable shrivelled morsel, not fit to eat. He carried his nuts partly in a big sack over his shoulder and partly in a large market basket. Somehow or other he managed to find room for a heavy pair of scales and these were always on the ground beside him by the time the women got to their front doors.

So, with his basket, his sack and his scales, Dicky went

THE PEDLAR OF MOLLAND CROSS

from door to door with pathetic perseverance rather than with brisk enthusiasm. It is quite a trek today by modern automobile along the metalled highway from Molland Cross to the shore of Barnstaple Bay. Sixty years ago this lover of the dusty track and hedgerow would be up before dawn and away. A story is told of him at work at Braunton Fair. He was selling two different kinds of nuts, one at 8d and the other at 10d lb. A city dweller out from Barnstaple for the day thought he would save himself twopence. After handing over his 8d and biting a couple, he could find nothing inside them. When he came back to make his complaint, Dicky chuckled, 'What do you expect, them's the swimming kind'. Part of the process of sorting out his nuts was to put them in a bowl of water. Those that rose to the top were bad or empty and these he would keep separate, to be sold, as we have seen, as the opportunity arose, to an unsuspecting urban gentleman more used to the bright lights and cobble pavement than the countryside and hedgerows. Dicky could size his customers up in a couple of moments. He could even tell from their speech what part of Devon they came from.

It quickly dawned upon him that if he could carry 56 lbs upon his back, and in his younger days he often carried this for many miles, then he could carry three times the weight and consequently sell three times as much if he acquired the services of a suitable four-legged animal. The Exmoor packhorse, so long a means of transport in this outback region of the Westcountry, was to him rather a cumbersome animal which lacked any sort of affection for its master. One day at South Molton, the Rev John Winnifrith, at that time rector of Mariansleigh, offered him one of his donkeys. 'Bred by the parson, so'ee must be proper,' was Dicky's comment. From that day onwards there grew up a warm friendship between Mr Winnifrith and the purchaser of his donkey and also between the donkey and his master. The affectionate association between man and workmate was to last over 20 years.

In his early pedlaring days, Richard Slader—'Mr Slader', as he liked to be called: he would tell one in no uncertain terms that he objected to being addressed as Dicky—would return early to his windswept cottage, and there would sit by his wood and peat fire, surrounded by his wares, penning his verses, cleaning his nuts for his trek on the morrow, and counting his takings of the day. Before retiring up the stairs, bare boards creaking under the weight of their owner, he would hang up his hat behind the door, kneel down in front of the stone hearth and say his prayers. His bed was of iron, with two heavy blankets and a pillow covered in serge. 'Devonshire serge,' he would say. 'Vicary serge of South Molton, dyed with Exmoor lichen.' (Vicary was one of the last firms to make serge in North Devon.) Sometimes it was difficult to recognise this as a bedroom. With its low whitewashed ceiling, its small window, a view the envy of all town dwellers, it would seldom be tidy, indeed it was very often difficult to find a place to tread. A pedlar's storeroom, whether in North Devon or a village of mud huts in steaming West Africa, is much the same concoction of colourful merchandise. Dicky was soon adding to his nuts such articles as chamber pots, and country vintages such as nettle pop, parsnip and potato wine, in addition to, in season, blackberries and sloes, taties, turnips, and such everyday farmhouse essentials as soap and candles. The occasional basket of eggs—'I know they's fresh, I laid 'em meself'—would be heaped on top of the chamber pots, 'very best porcelain, very hard wearing!'

His sheepdog would sleep on the dark cold flagstone, his donkey on a bed of straw in the adjoining weatherbeaten shelter of corrugated iron sheets; occasionally during a bitter winter's night, the blinding snow sweeping down from Five

Barrows, Dicky would have his 'hard-working helpmate' inside; the night would quietly pass until the faint glimmer of the dawn appeared over the grey silent moor. Only occasionally a rustle beyond the hedgerow would disturb the peace of the countryside; a fox or hind would scamper away, disturbed perhaps by an owl whose echoing cry carried far over the fields of the parish.

As the daylight began to filter across the eastern sky Dicky would be about. After cocoa for himself, dog and donkey, he would be on his way, perhaps across the frosty moor to Lynton, down the flooded Mole Valley to Chulmleigh, or just sauntering from farmhouse to farmhouse. High Bray to Charles, North Molton to Molland, North, South, East, and West, they all loved to see Dicky: the Welsh and the Durham miners having a pint of cider at the end of their shift; the shepherds and the farmers; the wives at home by the cottage door; they all reserved a welcome for the pedlar, his wares, his poems.

During the wet summer of 1903 he was returning home across the 'Chains' from Lynton after selling a basket of peas to one of the hotels there. (He had a good contact in Lynton; his nephew David was employed there at the stables attached to the Valley of Rocks Hotel, and from time to time during the summer, with the influx of visitors, he obtained quite a bit of business for him.) On this particular occasion the sky was darkening even before he had reached the Saddle Gate Stone. With the dark clouds threatening, the winds rising from the Sou'-West, the sheep scurrying for shelter, Dicky pressed on towards Moles Chamber. It wasn't long before the heavens opened, the thunder deafened and the lightning zigzagged across the black sky. It was a frightening experience and even when he reached his cottage door, the curtain of dusk just closing over the western horizon and the storm out of sight to the east, his face was still white, his hands still shaking. Richard collapsed in his chair, his jacket a mass of sodden matted wool, and gave thanks for his deliverance. That night he wrote a poem of thanks and afterwards whenever the subject turned to storms upon the moor Dicky would quote the first few lines of his composition.

One midsummer on his way back from Lynmouth he went by way of Oare—James Steer, Nicholas Snow's 'keeper, had some goslings for sale. By chance he came upon Nicholas Snow himself. Knowing that he had recently entertained King Edward VII at Oare Manor, he immediately started telling him all about his ancestry, his family's coat of arms, and tales of Sladers upon the moor centuries ago. 'I should be up in London with a crown 'pon me 'ead.' Dicky would often come up with this when conversation got around to royalty.

It was a few years earlier that, coming back from the Brendon Pony Fair along the old road to Parracombe, he had his startling encounter with John Mill Chanter, for 51 years cleric of Ilfracombe, who had taken the old Millslade Inn in the Brendon valley as a country retreat. The great bearded figure of Chanter, riding his Exmoor pony Heatherbell, apparently had strong effects on Dicky. 'Bless me, Chanter, I could have sworn it was Jesus riding upon His ass.' Afterwards whenever he met this or any other parson he would talk of this meeting upon the moor. 'Scared the wits out of me,' he would say. 'Never thought I would come across him on that lonely road. And there's not a chapel anywhere near there.' This last remark would often start a merry argument between Dicky and his Church of England friends; and this was just what he wanted.

At Barnstaple Fair one September he was introduced to Thomas Ruddle, B.A., the great Bible Christian educationist and headmaster of Shebbear College. Ruddle was amazed at his powers of memory, his knowledge of the Bible and the variety of subjects upon which he could converse. From his pocket Dicky pulled a bundle of dirty-looking papers. He knew immediately the one he was looking for—a hymn he had specially written for Bible Christians, set to the tune 'Marching on to war':

> Ho! all ye heavy laden,
>   Ye wanderers from God,
> There's shelter found in Jesus,
>   And pardon in His Blood.
> His wings are now expanded
>   To give the weary rest,
> To welcome home the mourner,
>   And clasp him to His breast.
>
> *Chorus*
> Oh, what a Friend is Jesus,
>   He always is the same;
> His Love is ever changeless,
>   And holy is His name!
> We find in Him redemption,
>   Through trusting in His blood,
> And by His Holy Spirit
>   He keeps us near to God.

On several occasions since leaving home brother Thomas had returned to North Molton and had always paid a visit to the little cottage at Molland Cross. Little did Richard realise that his visit during the June of 1903 was to be his last. He had come home to rest after a serious illness and returned to his chapel at Addiscombe in South London very much better. After a relapse on 20 November he passed away.

When Dicky heard the news he turned back home after setting out for South Molton, sat by his lonely fire and penned a poem, as he had done following the loss of his mother and father.

Although, dear Thomas, thou art gone,
   I love to think of thee,
And often say God's will be done,
   He is from pain set free.

Yes! pain and sickness are no more,
   And crosses all laid down,
And, on the bright Eternal Shore
   Thou hast received a crown.

And now before the Great White Throne
   In God's own house above,
Thou evermore wilt have a home
   Where Jesus Reigns in Love.

The Seraph Host are singing there
   'Glad songs' of endless peace,
With all the 'band of Angels fair',
   Whose praises never cease.

And twice ten thousand 'Saints in Light'
   Sweet praise to Jesus sing,
Who brought them to that home so bright,
   Their Saviour and their King.

And 'Thou dear Thomas', too, art there,
   Thy joys no tongue can tell,
These glories Thou wilt ever share,
   And in God's presence dwell.

Thy Brothers and thy Sisters, too,
   Remember thee in love,
And when from earth we have to go—
   Oh, may we meet above.

And, when before God's throne we meet,
   Where, Thomas, thou dost dwell,
We'll cast our crowns at Jesu's feet,
   Who 'doeth all things well'.

THE PEDLAR OF MOLLAND CROSS

This poem was subsequently printed by a friend, but, as he said whenever he composed a few lines on those who had departed, 'not to make money out of our loved ones who we shall not see again until we meet above. But of course, me dear, if you have a few coppers to exchange for such beautiful verses . . .' Sometimes he would place a few copies at the door of his chapel, and later as the congregation was leaving he would ask them one by one, 'Have yer paid the Lord for Richard's poems?' It was his way of doing a little to help the cause of Molland Cross. In time people came to recognise that when they saw some of Richard's printed poems on the table by the chapel door they would be expected to take one and make their payment in the collection plate.

Stories of Dicky spread far afield during the early years of the century. Summer tourists who had heard talk of him, from relations, from friends, or from those who had heard of him in the markets and inns around North Devon, would seek him out and have a chat with him. His dialect was typical of the Exmoor border country. It would give him great pleasure to have visitors and show them over his cottage and his wares. He made a great many friends and people would regularly call on him year after year to hear tales of his life. It was all so interesting to those town folk from up country.

FRIENDS AND NEIGHBOURS

> His name is fixed on rocks and rills
> Wrote by a Sacred pen;
> And in the valleys and on hills
> We see God's love to men.

AT this time South Molton had an enterprising photographer, Mrs Elizabeth Askew. For some years, helped by her sister, she had built up a good business amongst the aristocracy of these parts. She suggested when she saw Dicky one day in the Market that as he was such a smart man he ought to have his photograph taken for all the folks to see. Quickly the appointment was made and a few days later Dicky stayed in to await his visitors, who included Mrs Askew, her son and his wife, her sister and her husband, together with Mrs Askew's grandchildren and her housekeeper, Emma Thorne.

One of these grandchildren tells the story:

> When I and my sisters and brothers were children we were often brought to South Molton for holidays. On this occasion we were taken by horse and trap to Molland Cross. When we got there we found Dick sitting by his fire, sniffing up black pepper from the palm of his hand as he had a cold. My mother, who was very proud of our auburn hair, said, 'Well, Mr Slader, and what do you think of my daughters?' He looked up slowly and slyly replied, 'Well, Missus, they be all rid 'eaded anyway'. That has been a family joke ever since.

The cottage was in a real shambles that day. Mrs Askew's son and Miss Thorne had to brush some of the debris out of

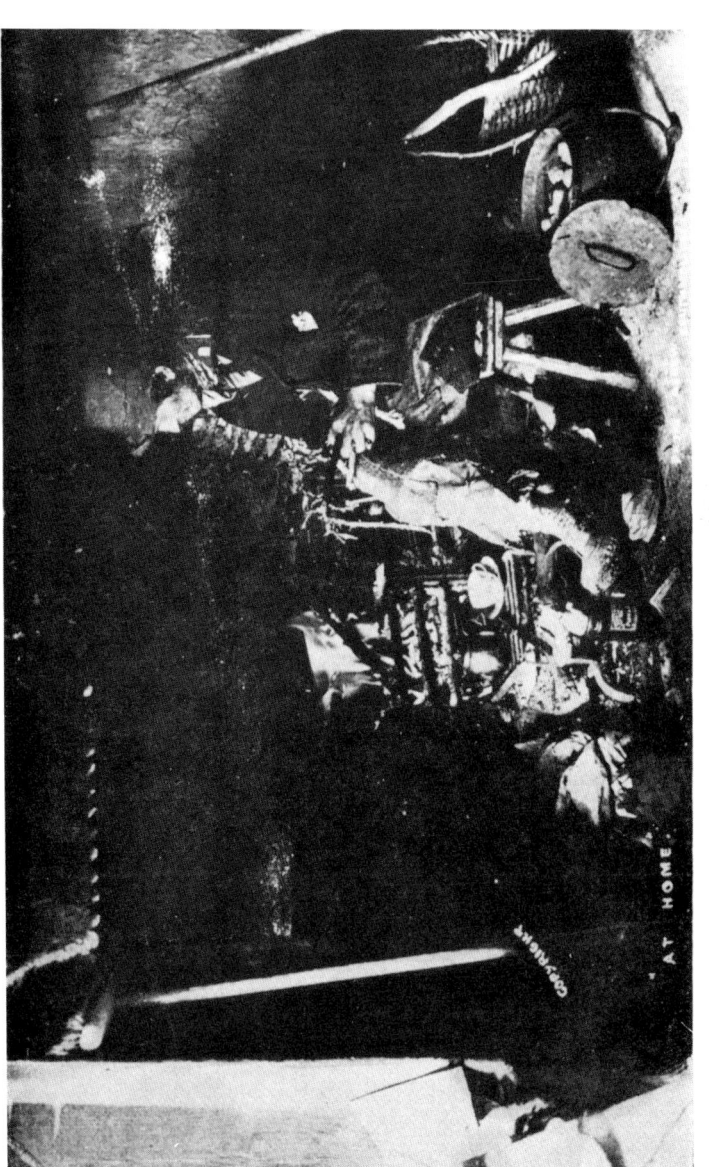

I. 'At Home'. The postcard that made him famous

II (top left). William Slader, his father   III (top right). Mary Ann Slader, his mother   IV (bottom left). Thomas Slader, his favourite brother (and grandfather of the author)   V (bottom right). Betsy, his favourite sister, with her husband, George Richardson of Manchester

VI. In his Sunday best

VII (top). His home for 30 years
VIII (bottom). In his garden

IX. Surrounded by his poultry

X. At his cottage gate

XI. With Colonel Hall, brother-in-law of Mrs Askew

XII. The outing to Ilfracombe. Dicky is in back row, sixth from right

the way to be able to photograph him. 'We also went up in his bedroom and saw all the little tables full of postcards what had been sent him from different people who had called to see him when on holiday.' After taking some photos by his fire they went outside to take more in the lane (with his chickens) and in the garden (with his hoe). This was the day that the celebrated 'At Home' photograph was taken, a snap of a kindly Devon countryman by his fireside which was to sell in hundreds during the course of the next few years at Mrs Askew's shop in South Molton. In those days tourists bought the picture as today they would buy 'a view of Exmoor'. They were bought, too, by local farmers' wives anxious to send a short message to a cousin up country or the seed merchant in Brayford. (These were the days before farms had telephones.)

As an old resident of South Molton recalls: 'A framed copy of this photograph hung in the house in which I was born. As a child I studied it on countless occasions.' Why was it that a photograph of an ordinary country pedlar should hold pride of place along with photographs of, no doubt, 'Aunt Susy's wedding', 'Young Master Jim in his new sailor's uniform', and 'Gran and Grandad on their Diamond Wedding Anniversary'? To the folks of South Molton and thereabouts Dicky was a little of their heritage, something to be talked about, something to be preserved in the days when Victorian England was being quickly left behind. A little of that past and of the old country travellers was preserved in him.

At harvest time Dicky would help at all the adjoining farms. He was very quick at tying corn, by hand with a twisted bond of straw; in fact few, if any, local men of that period could beat him at it. He was a frequent visitor at 'Walscott' just a short distance from his cottage, where Farmer Gould and his wife always kept a welcome for him.

He normally came either just before breakfast or just before supper. He was always given a meal, but would not sit at the table with the family, but always by a large open fire; and he seemed to prefer to squat on his haunches than to sit on a chair —and he seemed to be able to do this indefinitely without any sign of discomfort. He normally came to buy corn for his fowls, and his practice was to open the back door and begin calling out as he came along the passage, 'Maister, I want some corn —and yer's the money'. He always brought the cash with him. In return for helping with the harvest he was allowed to run his fowls over the stubble and place some of his fowl houses in the field for that purpose.

He rented a field known as 'Shallow Cleave' at £3 per annum from Mr Gould. Where the field adjoined the road was a tunnel known as a 'cattlecreep' to enable cattle to reach the field on the other side of the road without crossing it. This spot was known as 'Shallow Hill'. Richard blocked up one end of the 'creep' as a shelter for his pigs, but on one occasion they strayed on the road and he was fined 7s 6d for the offence. He composed 'The Molland Cross Song' concerning this incident, which he had printed and sold at a penny a copy to cover his fine. Needless to say he sold more than enough copies at South Molton Market a short time afterwards.

> Come, all you Farmers, stand around,
>   And hear me sing this song,
> For in our Village I have found
>   A man that's doing wrong.
>
> *Chorus*
>
> This man is often out around
>   To Farmers, and to all,
> To see if cattle can be found,
>   Or pigs come to his call.

FRIENDS AND NEIGHBOURS 35

> They call him 'Paddy Foster Blue',
>   He came out here one day,
> And said some things that are not true,
>   But what, I shall not say.
>
> Another day he pass'd this road,
>   Outside the Garden hedge,
> And up the Shallow hill he stroll'd
>   And stood upon the Bridge.
>
> He looked into the Bridge so dry,
>   But nought there could he reach,
> And see the pigs he could not buy
>   At seven-and-sixpence each.
>
> I'm singing this that you may know
>   What folks there are about;
> And very soon I mean to show
>   How things are working out.
>
> But, Farmers, don't be out of heart,
>   And Workmen, fear no wrong,
> For should he act the liar's part,
>   I'll make another song.
>
> I'll bravely stand for truth and right,
>   Though foes obstruct the way,
> For by God's grace, and in His might,
>   I'm sure to win the day.
>
> Then, Hail with me this Wondrous Grace,
>   Oh, Praise this Powerful Might,
> Which makes us bold our foes to face
>   And Victors in the fight.

Paddy Foster Blue referred to in the second verse was the name thinly disguising the local constable, P.C. Ireland. The chorus expresses Richard's allegations that the constable opened the gate and permitted the pigs to stray.

Dicky set the song to the tune 'Trelawney', and whether at the cottage door or at the market, surrounded by droves of sheep and bustling farmers, he would sing it for a copper or two. His voice and appearance would attract a crowd of spectators, and often ridicule and teasing from the young boys.

The books of F. J. Snell on the history of North Devon and some of its inhabitants, written during the first decade of this century, make interesting reading over 50 years later. In *The Blackmore Country*, published in 1906, Mr Snell records a visit to North Molton where he purchased a photograph of Dicky, dressed in his hat and frock-coat—another copyright by Mr Askew. This was the outfit he reserved for funerals only.

> As the topic is literature, I may here allude to a contemporary writer whose portrait I purchased in a shop opposite The Poltimore Arms. At the time I was quite ignorant of his precise claim to celebrity, and the silk hat, frock coat and walking stick were too conventional to suggest genius, though the face, perhaps, was not strictly normal. However, experience told me that no man would figure on a picture postcard unless possessed of unusual gifts, and it turned out that Mr Richard Slader was a poet and a solitary, whose recreations—to borrow the line from 'Who's Who'—consist in keeping a hundred head of poultry and selling blackberries at South Molton Fair. About 45 years of age, and careless of appearances, he might be taken, as somebody expressed it, for an old tramp, but he belongs to a respectable family; indeed, the name occurs in the Blackmore Pedigree. Moreover, it is known that his father left him a good round sum of money. Slader talks broad Devonshire and 'Richard and his pigs' have passed into a proverb. Swine have been a source of infinite worry to him. Certain of the species owned by his sister at Pixyweek became infected with anthrax and were ordered by the Police to be destroyed. This annoyed Mr Slader and he gave vent to his indignation in a poem. On another occasion he was

FRIENDS AND NEIGHBOURS

summoned for allowing his own pigs to stray on the highway, convicted and fined. Resentment at this petty tyranny led to his penning an effusion which was printed and circulated in a leaflet form.

Like all poets, Mr Slader has his critics and admirers. In a counter-leaflet put forth by some 'snake in the grass' he is revealed as the 'silly old man from South Molton', but the hiss of these ignoble strangers is as far beneath his polished verse as it is possible to conceive. It is proper to add that Mr Slader indited pathetic and very pious compositions on the deaths of his Mother and Sister.

Dicky's 'ole donkey' often caused him trouble with the neighbouring farmers. This intelligent beast was as artful as his master when it came to living by its wits. It fed totally on the hedges of the roadside, except when food was scarce and the fences were fairly easy to climb through after the leaves had fallen: then, somehow or other, the donkey would 'stray'. Dicky wasn't slow in turning a blind eye to its preference for other people's grass. He had a smug way of treating the farmers' protestations, and nobody was able to make him feel the wrong of his encroachments or trespassing. One farmer, annoyed by seeing the donkey so often in his fields, accosted Dicky with great warmth. 'The next time I see your old donkey on my fields, I'll shoot him dead on the spot,' he said.

'Aw do-ant'ee go duin' that there, Maister; do-ant'ee shut me ole donkey, Zur! I'd zooner vor'ee shut me a braace o' rabbats an' zen' me down!' Dicky's smooth tongue usually saved him. 'Aw yer, Varmer Jan, yu an' me us gaws tu the zame chapel. Yu wud'n grudge me pore ole donkaay a bit o' grass, wud'ee? Tull'ee wat now, I'll bring Missis up zum blackberries so's 'er kin make zum jam. Sure'n'uff I will. But doan'ee carry on zo, Varmer, about me pore ole donkaay. 'Eee woan du it agin, I promise'ee.'

This donkey, without which the image of Dicky would never be complete, became nearly as well known as his master. His name, always so affectionately called by Richard, and his full pedigree, was Eva Mini Mona Francis Adelaide Hamilton Jessie. Such a donkey, he would tell stranger or neighbour, had to have seven names: he came from a royal line of donkeys, and one of his ancestors was born in Jerusalem and belonged to Jesus Christ Himself. Indeed to prove his point Dicky would point out the mark of the cross on the animal's back (no doubt a branding mark). At Christmastime about dusk one could hear the donkey going clop, clop as he started for home from South Molton and Dick singing in the night air, 'Abide with me . . .' With the church bells ringing out in the background a serene picture of contentment he made.

Many a tale is told of the small boys in South Molton and their amusement at the antics of Eva Mini Mona . . . Dicky rode Arab fashion, sitting well back on the animal's rump— usually side-saddle, only there wasn't any saddle. 'Them blasted chillern', as he would call them, were for ever trying to raise fun out of him, and it was fairly easily done when two or three of them got together. On a couple of occasions he left his donkey outside the Devon and Cornwall Bank in South Molton (as far back as 1906 Richard kept his affairs in such an orderly fashion that he used a bank). The youngsters unhitched the donkey from the railings outside and dashed away before he came out. His dear companion would never wander without him, but nevertheless he was annoyed.

One day on the occasion of South Molton Fair, Dicky asked one of the clerks in the bank if he could bring his donkey in whilst he conducted his business. The clerk called the manager who, always wishing to oblige his clients, said, 'Certainly, bring him in, Mr Slader'. On such a day as this the

FRIENDS AND NEIGHBOURS

bank was crowded—gentlemen farmers, parsons, shopkeepers, farm bailiffs. They all knew Dicky and his donkey. However, the nuisance created made the clerks wish they'd never seen the animal. On many an occasion afterwards Dicky could be seen leading the donkey, complete of course with his basket and wares, into the bank or some of the shops in the market square.

A trick of the local boys was to hide behind a hedge as he was passing and pitch over some light harmless material such as a dry bit of stick or a ball of paper or a tiny pebble, very near him. A friend of Dicky's recalls just such an episode.

> I saw this tantalization going on one day under the skilful direction of two schoolboys, one on each side of the road. It was a long time before he discovered the direction whence the missiles came, but at last he caught sight of a boy's foot in the hedgerow. As he was not however capable of catching them or administering physical correction, his only chance was to lecture them in the vernacular: 'Yar! Yar now! Tell'ee wat now! Do-ant'ee go gwain doin' that there now! Yu'll vrighten me ole donkaay. Yu bess wy picky yer wy along now! Yu bess wy mitchy yer wy 'omeward!'

During the years following his father's death Dicky had more than once approached the Vicar of North Molton, the Rev H. M. Burdett, in an effort to record his father's passing in stone, for which he had specially composed a piece of poetry. These lines, however, were never worked by the local mason for Dicky objected to paying the small fee, the common dues of God's Acre. 'Aw, yar now! yu didn' aught tu charge nothin', yu know. Me vather waz churchwardin of this yer parish, an' he drawed all them there sto-ans for restorin' the old church vor nort, yu know,' he told the vicar. 'Right!' replied the rather sharp Burdett, 'If that be so, then it is enough to make the good old man turn in his grave for his son to be so mean as to object to pay the common dues of God's Acre.' In due course the stone was erected but, no doubt to save a few coppers in mason's fees, without the verses. Parson Burdett's father had christened Dicky and several of his brothers and sisters. 'Never like his father,' was Dicky's comment. Richard had been in the habit of attending the parish church on special occasions, top hat, white gloves, and fingers glistening with rings of what seemed to be a multitude of stones.

The year 1912 can be considered a milestone in the career of Mr Richard Slader. At 55 he could no longer be considered a young man, and yet the following 14 years were to be as eventful as the 14 that had just passed. The period began with 'The Molland Cross Robbery'.

MOORLAND EXPLOITS

> I give my time and talents too,
> That I may be a soldier true;
> And by His side in garments white,
> I tread the path that leads to light.

THE Molland Cross Robbery will be recorded in the annals of this hamlet for all time. Like so many legends of this neighbourhood—one immediately recalls to mind those of Tom Faggus and Sir Ensor Doone—it has become exaggerated over the years. The Rev W. W. Joyce, rector of Charles during this period, and a friend of Dicky's, dwells upon this incident in his tale of 'Urchard' (the Exmoor pronunciation of Richard) while using his own imagination to a certain extent. (*Echoes of Exmoor*. Second Series. Chapter 3.)

As can be imagined, Dicky's way of life over the years had caused a certain amount of gossiping between the locals as to what he was doing with all his money. Fabulous stories of his secret wealth grew up: that there was hardly a stick of furniture, a niche or corner in wall or floor or roof that did not contain bags of gold and silver; that the cottage was literally lined with coins, and that the weight of precious metal hidden away was more than the masonry and timbers of the cottage itself. The stories became the talk of Exmoor and soon the rumours were heard in circles that were not so law-abiding as his neighbours.

It so happened that two stalwart and ruffianly-looking tramps started simultaneously one morning, the one from

Lynton, the other from South Molton, and they met somewhere by chance near Molland Cross. They compared notes of the neighbourhood, and both had heard of the supposed riches of 'this old miser'. Mysteriously, Dicky's poor noisy sheepdog died that night, 'poisoned by them blasted ruffians', as he said later. At the time, however, Dicky thought he had been taken by old age and his sudden loss depressed him. After making a rough wooden coffin, he laid 'best pal old Richard could ever have' to rest in his garden, and was consoled by the fact that his donkey 'would not let him down'.

A couple of days afterwards the two tramps met outside the cottage door just as darkness was falling. Lying under cover, they heard Dicky shut in his poultry and enter the house, closing the door behind him. Before he had time to settle down, the latch was lifted, the door was swung open, and the two powerful-looking fellows, 'girt big god-fearing devils', as Dicky said, stood before him. One seized him and stopped his mouth with his flat hand, another swung round his face a long thick woollen scarf, winding it about his mouth so as completely to gag speech or sound. One of the men held a bar of iron in his hand, and as they tied him to the settle, they gave him to understand that if he tried to move or make a noise, one blow would deprive him of life, while if he remained quiet and assisted them he would escape without further injury.

Though they ransacked the cottage from roof to floor and hastily filled their bags, they were disillusioned as to the extent of their victim's wealth. They made off, leaving Dicky strapped to the settle and gagged with the scarf. There he remained till about 10 o'clock the next day, when a farmer called to ask about his dog. He set him free, lit his fire, and heard the story while helping him to get some food. Immediately Dick was away to North Molton police station. Since the publication of The Molland Cross Song and the episode at 'Shallow Cleave', he didn't get along well with Paddy Foster, the local policeman. For several years he had been telling everyone that he and Foster were no friends; "Bout time they moved him from this parish'. Nevertheless the law was quickly at work. 'Maybe git you promotion,' Dicky said, rubbing his hands with glee at the thought of a new bobby.

True enough, the law got their men. One was arrested at Simonsbath and the other, who escaped by Charles and East Buckland, at Swimbridge. Some silver and notes were found upon each. They were brought to South Molton for trial, and Dicky was there to give evidence. Only one of the criminals was of local origin. Dicky said he knew his brother, and that 'They waz all a rough lot. His brother could ait whit-pot till he could touch it with 'is vinger, an' drink zider till it urn'd out bo-ath zides of 'is mouthe!'

'Where did the bags of money lie at the time of the burglary?' asked the magistrate.

'Up (sniff) in me baid-drawin'-room (sniff), up there!' whined out Dicky, in sobs.

'At what time of day was it?'

'A'bowt (sniff) a quarter arter dark (sniff), I reckon (sniff), up in me baid-drawin'-room, up there!' (Sniff.)

'And how much money do you think you had there altogether?'

'Dree 'undred an' dree 'alf-crowns (sniff), tu 'underd an' nine shillin's and twenty-vive pound no-ats, an' the rest waz coppers. Tell'ee wat now!' said Dicky, recovering his spirits somewhat as he went on reckoning.

It took Dicky some months to get over this episode and every night he took care to secure his door. He missed Sammy his sheepdog, his faithful friend for over 14 years, and once told a neighbour that he could never replace him.

It was during this period that he went around the neighbourhood attending Harvest Festivals and anniversaries at the Wesleyan chapels. The weeknight service at North Molton became another attraction, and not a Tuesday would pass without Dicky in his place immediately in front of the minister. On all such occasions he would, of course, be attired in top hat and white gloves. He quickly rebuked an acquaintance who addressed him one Sunday at Heasley Mill chapel as 'Richard', saying he was 'Mr Slader' on Sundays. One winter Tuesday evening at North Molton, Dicky remained on after the service to enjoy the heat from the stove. By accident he put his hand on the stove but quickly withdrew it. Looking at his hand, he remarked to those who sat around, 'Do'ee think hell will be as hot as that?'

'Yes, according to scripture,' said Mr Treble, who was always anxious to engage Mr Richard in conversation.

'I shall never be able to stick it,' replied Dicky.

Several of his compositions were sung to well-known tunes at Wesleyan missions in North Devon. At the various chapels the contributions of this 'local' were something of an event and greatly admired by visiting ministers. A typical example of his work was 'Lines on the Coming Mission', which he specially composed for the Wesleyan Methodist church at North Molton and which he set to the tune 'Jerusalem the Golden'. A hymn of considerable length, its first two verses make clear the message he was trying to give.

> Dear Reader, speak to Jesus,
>   Ask Him to make you glad,
> Get ready for the Mission—
>   With Holiness be clad.
>
> There's work within God's vineyard
>   For one and all to do;
> The harvest now is plenteous,
>   And labourers are few.

Those who recall this Exmoor character as an eccentric yokel generally refer to this period of his life. Instances come to light which show he was at times a little odd in his behaviour, no doubt due to the very lonely life which he led. All his close relations had now left the parish and whilst he had his visitors in the summer months, the winters were long and dreary. When the icy cold winds blew down from Five Barrows capped with the January snowfall; when the fields of a February morn across the parish to Yard Gate glistened with crispy frost; when even his neighbours seemed to forget his existence, Dicky would sometimes feel a little forlorn. He would love to leave his cottage and away to market, to mix, to chat, to sing, and to watch the fascinating scene.

The pedlar of old still pursued his trade. To lighten his burden he had a small cart made which he harnessed to his donkey. To a stranger at Heasley Mill who one day asked him whether his poor donkey could manage the steep hill leading up from the Mill, he replied, 'Me donkey's not so poor as you think and you can tell by his eyes he's not as old as I am. Anyhow,' went on Dicky, 'even when he is poor, old and blind he'll still follow his maister home, them's no strangers, you know.'

The picture of him attending the funeral of Mrs Askew, the photographer, who died in 1912, gives us an insight into his inner self. In his accustomed dress for such occasions he followed the funeral procession, tail coat, top hat, carrying a black-edged handkerchief. With his small pocket Bible in his hand he stood at the edge of the grave, close relations of the deceased standing by. With the leaves of autumn falling, with the parson quietly intoning the last rites, Dicky gently touched his eyes with his handkerchief and murmured a few inaudible words to the departed one. When those that had gathered had left the graveside, Dicky turned to them and offered a few words of comfort. Dick would travel far for the funeral of an acquaintance, to pay his last respects 'until we meet again standing together before the Great White Throne', as he would say. To Lynton, Simonsbath, even to Barnstaple he would go, to stand in the graveyard, sun, rain or snow, clutching his black-edged handkerchief, bare-headed with top hat in hand. To the mourners he would often quote one of his small verses:

> This earthly life of ours will soon be past,
> Then, only what was done for Christ will last.

Being unwell one day, Dicky went to see the doctor at South Molton and described to him the nature of his ailment. After prescribing the correct medicine the doctor was interrupted by his patient muttering something about the hurry he was in and how he must get back home. As he was going out of the surgery door Dicky called out, 'Thank'ee, Doc, and if I should ever become ill I promise 'ee will be my doctor.'

As elsewhere in the neighbourhood, the children of Heasley Mill would love to gather around him to hear him talk and tell his yarns. One day there by the Mill where he had come to collect some pig meal, he asked the children who knew the most, their school teacher or him. When they replied 'The teacher', he was very upset, taking up his stick to reinforce his protest. The children ran for the school, followed closely by Dicky. When they got inside, the teacher, seeing them out of breath and their clothes untidy, looked out of the window to see if she could ascertain the reason for all this commotion. There was Dicky lying against the wall crying.

On Whit Mondays he would make a very early start for Combe Martin as he estimated that here he could make an extra ten shillings on this particular day. By sunrise he would be passing through Brayford, sitting side-saddle with his donkey laden with two large baskets of eggs. After leaving Kentisbury behind he would drop down into Combe Martin's narrow street long before 9 o'clock. This quiet village, which once produced more silver from its mines than all the rest of the kingdom put together, would hardly be astir. With the sun just rising above Great Hangman, with the great bells of the church ringing out over the valley, as was the custom in those days at Whitsuntide, the houses and shops would slowly come to life. Amidst this peaceful atmosphere, still at that date undisturbed by the internal combustion engine, was Dicky, now dismounted, leading his friend. Greeting everyone he met, he made his way to the small quay, where lapped the waves of the calm Severn Sea. All morning he would blow his horn—a type of hunting horn given him by the Master of the Exmoor Foxhounds—calling 'New-laid eggs, laid 'em all myself', and indulging in much witty sales talk. By noon he would be sold out and start to make his way homewards. He once said that the people of Combe Martin kept a very tight rein on their purse strings and that Whit Monday was the only day of the year he could make any money there.

Outside the regular weekly markets and such occasions as Barum Fair, Bampton Fair and Brendon Pony Fair, Lynton and Lynmouth were his favourite spots. Various memories of him at this time remain. Once he sold one of his pigs to a Lynton butcher and with a bucket of corn he coaxed it all the way from Molland Cross, across the moor and through Barbrook. Another day, as he went to Lynton, it was raining heavily such as it can on 'The Chains'. Dicky took his coat off and put it over his bucket of eggs to keep them dry. When he arrived, the shopkeeper who had ordered them looked at the bedraggled Dicky, the rain seeping from his shirt and trousers, and asked him why he had taken his coat off. Answered Dicky with a sly wink, 'Now I have a dry coat to wear'.

Coming down Lynton Hill one day, Eva Mini, the donkey, now getting on in years, missed his footing on the slippery surface. A basket of eggs, which Dicky was about to deliver to Bevan's Lyn Valley Hotel, smashed all over the road. Dicky could not help seeing the humorous side to his mishap, remarking to a passer-by, 'Damn me, they'd make a real good cake'. Eva Mini came out of the mishap best of all as Dicky made him eat up all the mess. The only thing he was concerned about was how much it had cost him to feed his donkey that day.

Another tale is told of Richard leaving his donkey at home one day and setting off on a brisk walk into South Molton. He was stopped by a car, the driver asking him whether he would like a lift. Up clambered Dicky into the seat beside the driver, not thinking to ask which way he was going. After they had gone a few miles he could see no sign of South Molton although he was keeping his weather eye open in between snatches of conversation. Eventually, after attracting the driver's attention to his plight, he got out, only to find he had further to walk to town than if he hadn't accepted the lift. A few days later he set off again by 'Shanks's pony' for South Molton. Again a car stopped and he was offered a lift into market. 'No, thank'ee,' said Dicky. 'I'm in a hurry.'

It was said on several occasions that certain ladies of the parish cast their eyes in the direction of Dicky. But Dicky had other ideas and remained single. He was once heard to say, 'Those that I do want to marry won't, and them that does want to marry me I don't want'. One particular lady in her forties, who used to make a practice of walking with him from chapel, actually asked him one day if he would like to marry her. It is said he never spoke to her again. He would say about plain women that 'they be better drove than led'. He meant, of course, that it was better not to see their faces.

1914-1918 AND AFTERWARDS

> The seed-time and the harvest show
> The wondrous love of God;
> The heat and cold, the rain and snow,
> He sends upon the sod.

JUST before the first world war, with the increase of summer tourists in the neighbourhood Dicky discovered that he could buy ginger beer in South Molton for 1d a bottle and sell it outside his cottage, or on his travels, for 3d or even 4d on a hot day.

One day a wealthy-looking gentleman was passing the cottage at Molland Cross, a stranger who appeared to have come a long way. Being a hot day in June and his visitor looking conveniently thirsty, Dicky asked him if he'd like a drink of ginger beer. 'Thank you, sir, that would be most welcome,' replied the rider, getting down from his horse. After he had refreshed himself he asked Dicky how much. 'Oh, that'll be all right, Squire,' he said, hoping of course that his important-looking visitor would at least bring 6d out of his pocket. 'That's very nice of you, my friend.' After passing remarks about the weather and the good crop of hay just cut in the field opposite, horse and rider prepared once more for the road. All the time Dicky was saying, 'Glad you enjoyed the drink, sir,' and 'A nice drop of ginger beer is so refreshing.' With no more ado the rider was on his way. Dicky took to his legs and caught him up towards Yard Gate. 'Nice drop of ginger beer,' said Dicky. 'This sort of weather you can do with a nice refreshing drink.' He tried hard to keep his visitor in conversation and turn the subject around to payment for his services. Unfortunately the lone rider took him at his word in the first place and was soon out of sight towards Moles Chamber. 'A proper rascal,' was Dicky's comment.

At this time Mr Richard Huxtable, of Brayford, who supplied Dicky with much of his corn and meal for his poultry, came to know him very well. Many a day he would call at the Huxtable house for a cup of tea. He was insistent on being heard, even when at times his host was busy with other things and did not wish to have to stop to talk. He would keep talking louder and louder until one had to listen. Often he would be given a cup of tea by Mrs Huxtable, who would then go about another job. Her daughter, coming in and seeing Dicky there, would say, 'Would you like some tea, Dicky?' And he would say, 'Thank'ee, I could do with a cup of tay,' and have it all over again.

One day at Brayford he called for a sack of maize. Putting his donkey and cart in the gateway, he went inside for his usual chat. Upon his return he found that some of the young lads of the village, for ever wanting to get a bit of fun out of him, had unhitched the donkey and put him inside the gate with the shafts of the cart through the gate and hitched to the donkey. He came running to Mr Huxtable in terrible trouble. 'Help! Help! Come quick and get me out!' On another occasion he called for a cup of tea and the brandish, a three-legged support for holding the large pans of jam, etc., over the fire, happened to be in the hearth. It was a cold day and wanting to get as close to the fire as possible, Dicky sat down on this. Up he quickly got, 'Oh, he's hot, he's hot, I'm burning, Mrs Huxtable, I'm burning,' he cried out. Many a time after this when he was asked to sit close to the fire he would answer, 'He's too hot, he's hot, missus'.

1914-1918 AND AFTERWARDS

John Huxtable, the North Devon wrestler in Blackmore's *Clara Vaughan*, was based upon the blacksmith at High Bray during the middle of the 19th century, a big, burly figure of a man and one of Richard Huxtable's forefathers. This fascinated Dicky and on many occasions he would draw attention to it and to his own connection with the Blackmore family. Another opportunity to do this arose at 'The Ring of Bells' in the village of Challacombe one day, when Dicky got into conversation with a local farmer by the name of John Ridd. Now the Ridds had farmed Challacombe and the adjoining parish of Bratton Fleming since the early 16th century, and one of them, of Leworthy, was the original character upon which Blackmore based his John Ridd of *Lorna Doone*. Mr Ridd, who knew Dicky by sight, although he had never met him before, was amazed by Dicky's 'You be a Ridd, I guess. Can tell'ee apart anywhere.' And so the conversation turned to the ancient families of the neighbourhood and the old legends surrounding them. As they parted company on this day and Dicky led his donkey up over Challacombe Common by way of Whitefield Barton, John Ridd just couldn't make out how this travelling salesman knew he was one of the Ridds. The incident illustrates Richard's remarkable powers of memory and recollections for faces. Having seen many of the Ridd family before, at markets, perhaps at chapels and churches of the district, on the moor and on the by-roads, he carried in his mind a recollection of the family likeness. Not only did Dicky know the birthdays, Christian names, dates of marriage and home of very many inhabitants of the Exmoor border country, but he could also roll off these details for most of the royal family, not only those alive at that time but back into history for over a century, for most of the politicians of the day, well-known preachers and the lesser-known civic dignitaries of such places as Barnstaple and Ilfracombe.

The first world war left Dicky unmoved. The trenches of France, the depths of the Atlantic, were so entirely different and far away from that quiet world that Dick called his own amongst the foothills of the moor. Whilst he was too old to be considered for military service he would make every effort to discourage others from going. He disagreed with the government of the day and the political leaders and had a strain of pacifism in him. He disliked force of any kind. Walking home from North Molton chapel one summer evening shortly after the *Lusitania* had been sunk, one of his younger companions said he couldn't stand any longer being left at home with so many of his own age serving king and country. He was going to join up. Dicky stopped short in his track. 'Do'nee go. Do'nee go. When you come back, you can go "up the hedge" for all they care.' How true this comment came to be in so many cases.

During these ageing years his neglect of his dress was becoming more and more apparent and to the unsuspecting stranger he appeared rather a dirty eccentric tramp, better kept at a distance rather than engaged in conversation. But he was full of humorous chit-chat, much of it still remembered by those who knew him. Upon returning from the dentist after having a tooth extracted and calling on friends in North Molton for a cup of tea, he produced the tooth from his pocket and held it in the palm of his hand. 'Do'ee think it'll ache any more?' he said. Another day, entering the village stores in his tattered jacket and trousers with a shirt so patched it looked like a patchwork quilt of many colours, he produced a sovereign, a very grimy one, in payment for his few groceries. As the young woman serving was casting a doubtful eye on the coin, he said, 'You needn't be afeared of 'un, missy. It's only a bit vinedy and if you let me 'ave it I'll rub it up and down me breeches a time or two.'

1914-1918 AND AFTERWARDS

The annual Molland Cross chapel outing to Ilfracombe—occasionally to Lynmouth—was a notable event in this rural society. It was not until 1916 that Dicky had been persuaded to join 'the seaside mob', as he called it. Everyone was relieved to note that he dressed up, and he was highly amused at the remark by one younger member of the party that he was getting gay and gadding about in his old age. But down on the beach on this particular occasion he was deeply concerned. It was the first time he had witnessed the 20th century tourist away from factory and city office. For the quiet country yokel that he was, still virtually living in the 19th century, with rather narrow-minded nonconformists as his neighbours and customers in this outback corner of North Devon, it came as a shock to be suddenly confronted with factory girls from Birmingham and London, boldly parading in bathing costumes and showing so much of themselves to complete strangers. Poor Dicky was further put out when some of the youngsters of Brayford invited him to join them for a dip in the sea. 'Never washed myself all over in me life,' he said. 'Not going to start down there now. Never had my body under water all at once and I never shall. Not for five pounds would I do it.' For weeks afterwards he would relate to all his customers 'them goings on in Ilfracombe. 'Twill lead to no good. Mark my words.'

Attending one of the local annual sales during the last year of the war, Dicky was heard to say to a neighbour as the people were dispersing, 'Wull, I s'poase I bes-way picky me way 'omeward. I do-ant zee no mo'er vo'ks up yer——'

'Ees there be,' broke in his neighbour. 'There be plenty o'volks abowt eet! Dissn'zee men?'

'Neet vor tell way,' concluded Dicky, as he sauntered out of the gate. This saying has since passed into a proverb and up until recently around the parishes bordering upon the western slopes of Exmoor, if a place was particularly lonely and out of the way, a reason for leaving it was found in: 'I do-ant zee no vo'ks yer vor tell way!'

Like many country people he was bilingual. He could speak embarrassingly correct English when addressing a visiting minister or talking to visitors from up country at Lynton. Yet he could relapse automatically into equally perfect vernacular when talking to his own friends and relatives, or selling his wares in the market place.

The war years quickly passed by and once the local lads were demobbed, it was Dicky who was the first to welcome them back home to the old parish. They were pleased to see his cheery rosy face; it was now difficult to imagine this corner of dear old England without the pedlar and his constant companion, his donkey.

In the parliamentary election of 1918 South Molton again returned George Lambert for the Liberal cause. It was on this occasion that Dicky Slader nearly landed himself in goal.

On the 'eve of the poll' Dicky made his way into South Molton anxious to hear the orators who were due to speak in the square. It so happened that he met some friends who were in town from the outlying farms, and it wasn't long before Dicky, quite against his will, found himself in the George Hotel. As can be imagined, this was a hectic night. All sorts of characters were in town, people that hadn't seen each other since before the war, money was plentiful, and before long it was politics in the bar rather than in the square. After joining his friends in a couple of pints of cider and being pressed to accept a double brandy which had appeared out of the blue, Dicky refused to accept any more. 'You'll be 'aving me muddle-'eaded 'avore I git 'ome. You can put the brandy in a bottle, it'll do me more good when I git 'ome.' The sequel to this revelry was that before the night was out the innocent

Dicky found himself, with ruffians the worse for drink, being escorted by the police towards the iron gates of South Molton gaol. The police, rather new recruits out in force on this election night, did not quite realize whom they had netted. Directly the guard at the gate saw who it was he freed Dicky at once. 'No need to hold him. He couldn't cause any trouble.'

The year 1920 is remembered as the time that Dicky lost his donkey. He died rather suddenly one frosty winter's night, certainly not of being neglected, most probably of old age and the intense cold. Dicky's comment was, 'He never served me that trick before'. The Rev W. W. Joyce, in his *Echoes of Exmoor*, describes a fantastic scene in which some mischievous schoolboys found the donkey feeding on the road side one day, and drove him off towards the Bray Valley where eventually, after Dicky had searched the area for several days, the donkey fell to his death over a quarry face. The scene records the end of 'Urchard' himself, for he had caught up with his donkey and was actually hanging on to the end of the rope when the donkey pulled him over as well. This fiction Joyce incorporated into his story to give added interest to his 'Urchard'. It was published whilst Dicky was very much alive.

Dicky's fame now spread to the variety stage, and he would appear at local concerts where he would recite his poetry, dressed in his rags and tatters, to the delight of all. He was 'billed' amongst Westcountry celebrities at a concert at South Molton put on by a local bank manager, and caused considerable amusement to the local populace.

Early in the '20s Dicky was beginning to feel his years. He was no longer as energetic as he had been although one could still see him crossing the moor on a frosty morning or walking into South Molton on market day, wet or fine, snow or sunshine. With his donkey gone he lightened his load considerably but as this limited his earning capacity and there were busy market days when he would be sold out by 10 o'clock, he would return to Molland Cross for a further basket of eggs or blackberries, to enable him to continue selling till the last folks had departed. Invariably he would then call at one of his relations who insisted he should have one decent hot meal every week.

During the summers, when the hot sun blazed down on the parched moorland, Dicky would often be out on Fyldon Common picking whortleberries. His 'territory', he said, was from Moles Chamber to Sandyway Cross. 'The best whorts in Devon. Pick 'em in me own 'at so ems mus' be clean,' he would say.

Although he refused to accept the approach of old age there were many who saw him at this time who knew that the closing years of his life were upon him. Nevertheless he still had ample opportunities to write his verses, to make new friends, to mourn the loss of others, to attend his chapel and his market and, above all, to recall the wonderful years through which he had lived. His memory of his own childhood and the days when he grew up were perfect images which if he had only transferred to paper would have made a fascinating story.

ALONE WITH HIS MEMORIES

> Keep us evermore, we pray,
> In the straight and narrow Way,
> Guide us by the Light of grace
> Till we reach God's dwelling place.

LORD and Lady Poltimore had often called at Dicky's cottage when they were passing by. They had a great respect for this sole survivor in the parish of a great North Molton family. Lady Poltimore and he would on occasions sit and talk for many hours together. Richard could give a little of the very essence of the English countryside, a down-to-earth picture of Devon and Devonians, which had perhaps escaped the squirearchy. He had known three generations of Poltimores and knew intimately the three sons that he had seen grow up at Court Hall. This great Jacobean mansion standing majestically just east of the church had fascinated Dicky since he was a small boy, and many a time he would stand outside the porch gazing up at the ancient stonework, pondering over the history of its fabric and the great family of Bampfyldes. Often during these years Lady Poltimore would tidy up the little cottage at Molland Cross and patch or mend if she could see that Dicky's clothes needed a little attention. Lady Margaret Poltimore was of high birth herself, being the daughter of Baron Allendale. Never again in these islands will the opportunity arise for two such people as these to sit and chat on the settle by the log fire.

For some reason relations between Dick and his near

neighbour, Mr Cook, became strained and had been so for some time when Mr Cook retired and prepared to leave the area. Bidding his last farewells after chapel one Sunday morning, Dicky said, 'I be sorry you be leaving us'. His neighbour, anxious not to part with swords drawn, explained, 'I don't believe you really are, Mr Slader, but I accept your concern'. Dicky said to one of the company as they were parting ways, 'In two or dree weeks time they'll forget all about 'un, but they'se ul'be tellin' abou' me years to come.' How right he was.

In 1924 Richard lost one of his best friends, John Williams, who, though living in Cardiff, was a relation of one of Dicky's neighbours and often came over to stay, particularly during the summer. How much he valued his friend is best shown by his letter to Mr Huxtable, which like all his letters was penned in a most polished manner.

My Dear Mr. Huxtable,

I am sending you and Mrs. Huxtable some of my Beautiful verses.

Perhaps you will oblige me with keeping them in very dear memory of my Ever Dearest Friend, the late Mr. Williams, Watchmaker and Silversmith, who was the eldest son of Mr. James and Mrs. Williams of Welshpool.

He was born on the 28th day of January in the year of Our Lord 1865 and died in his home at 57 Crwys Road, Cathays, Cardiff. He was a real good man, but his Death came as a very great surprise and shock to me. About four weeks before, all at once he was taken very poorly, and as he did not improve a Specialist was called, who discovered he was suffering of Cancer in the stomache, which became very painful.

No one will ever know what suffering he passed through the last fortnight of His life. Oh! I wish I could have been with him the *whole* of the time. I can never forget him. But now, he is where no blight or darksome showers can ever come, and weariness and pain are forever gone away; and all is peace, and joy, and *right*.

ALONE WITH HIS MEMORIES

For Evermore.
'My loss is his Eternal gain.'
He is very near the 'Throne of God', where Jesus reigns in realms of endless '*right*', and pain, care—are for ever unknown.

I may say that my Friend leaves a wife and one Daughter, aged 22 years. But, Mr. Huxtable, you will be pleased to know that both May and Mother are very brave, their trust is in The Living God and He is all sufficient, and with His grace I trust that some day you and Mrs. Huxtable will see my '*Friend*' standing with myself before The Great White Throne. In the presence of The ONE Who gave *Himself* for us. Please accept this—combined—with the keeping of The Beautiful Verses.

From Yours in *Jesus*
Richard Slader.

Dicky had his verses printed in the usual way and several copies were distributed in the neighbourhood. It was his way of paying his last respects.

My dearest John, I think of thee
  Up in God's Home above,
From sorrow, care and pain set free,
  Where Jesus reigns in Love.

That happy home with portals fair
  And Mansion ever bright,
And God the Holy Ghost is there,
  Oh what a blessed sight.

The seraph Host and Angel being,
  Waft music on the air,
And up the Hallelujah strand
  Are Living Waters fair.

My dearest John, oh what a home,
  How beautiful the sight,
To see the Saviour on the throne
  In realms of endless Light.

> Glad songs of praise; they ever sing
>   All worthy is the Lamb,
> To be our Saviour, Lord and King,
>   And holy is his Name.
>
> And Dearest John the Holy Ghost
>   Shall be my constant guide,
> Until I meet that shining Host
>   Beyond the swelling tide.
>
> Then I shall go straight up to thee
>   And by thy side will stand,
> Where Christ our Saviour we can see
>   And praise at his Command.

The following year Dicky did not enjoy the best of health, and on many a day he was confined to his cottage which had now been his home for nearly 30 years. All alone he would sit and think, disturbed only by the postman, who still used to deliver letters and cards from admirers, and by close friends. During the nicest weeks of that hot summer he again ventured across the silent moor to Lynton, and he again sold his nuts and blackberries at South Molton market. To the youngsters he would now often adopt a wise guardian attitude, offering advice to all those that had little knowledge of the pitfalls and burdens of life. He still rarely missed his chapel and his hymn singing was as hearty as ever. His life, although rapidly drawing to its close, with the diabetes rapidly gaining control of his system, was, as it had always been, one of complete happiness and satisfaction.

On Christmas morning Dicky as usual walked the two miles to worship at the parish church in North Molton, barely eight weeks before he was confined to his bed for the last time. He himself knew it was the last time he would be able to attend this service and took great satisfaction in telling everyone this

ALONE WITH HIS MEMORIES

news. His friends found it difficult to believe, but he insisted it was true and that he had been told by Christ the King who was already preparing a place for him. To the stranger he was a crank, but to friends who had known him a lifetime this was the true Dicky, a great believer, a man of faith, a sincere man who spoke his feelings. Many of them later that Christmas Day wondered whether possibly he did know that his departure from the parish and the people that he loved was close at hand.

Over three weeks before his life closed, the following April, he predicted the actual day and hour of his death. He also chose the bearers of his coffin and gave instructions as to how his funeral was to be conducted. For his chapel at Molland Cross he handed over a certain amount of money to the stewards which he insisted be used to erect a brass tablet recording his life and his service to the Wesleyan cause.

His passing is best recorded by an extract from the *North Devon Gazette* of 24 April 1926.

> There passed away on Tuesday a figure long familiar throughout this district in the person of Mr. Richard Slader of Molland Cross. His originality and exceptionally retentive memory—he was never at a loss for the birthday or wedding day of any member of the Royal Family, and could recite the chief events in the history of many prominent people with remarkable accuracy—made him an outstanding personality.
>
> Living in an isolated locality, close to Exmoor, Mr. Slader was never better pleased than when a visitor chanced to look in. He followed current events carefully, and his opinions, though often quaintly phrased, shewed much keenness of perception. As a young man, he sang tenor tolerably well, and in 1892, when he resided at 'Hunawins' Farm, North Molton, published a readable booklet of verses. A photograph shewing Mr. Slader sitting by his hearth, surrounded by market goods, is familiar to most folk here-about, and holiday-makers visiting Exmoor were eager to secure a copy of the picture.

Mr. Slader was in the habit of walking to South Molton, Lynton, Barnstaple, and other markets, and must often have returned home over the moorland road in the small hours of the morning. He lived alone, and took special pleasure in shewing his household goods to callers. In order to hear visiting speakers, whether preachers or politicians, he tramped all over the district at one time or another, and could give an outline of a speech years after he had heard it.

At his funeral, the bearers were six neighbouring farmers, friends who respected Dicky as the last great countryman of North Devon. They gathered at his cottage on a bright spring morning, with only the noise of their horses' hooves disturbing the quiet of the countryside. They rode in front of the hearse to North Molton. They carried him into the church. They carried him to his last resting place beside his father and mother.

> Then, when landed on the shore
> Of that home so fair,
> I shall sing for evermore,
> And dwell with Jesus there.

In contrast to his usual well-disciplined ways, Dicky had omitted to draw up his will—an indication that he had little to leave. Yet when he had been taken with his last illness, a local woman engaged to look after him had much upset him by starting to clean his cottage, and by burning in the garden a lot of rubbish; he had realized what was going on, although his illness had prevented him from making people understand what he was upset about. Afterwards local gossip, as is so often the case, attributed his distress to the fear that hidden savings were being burnt: be that as it may, it was a fact that after his effects were auctioned, the purchaser of his grandfather clock found a sum of money hidden in it, which was afterwards returned to the personal representatives. This was, however, the sole instance of 'buried treasure'. His distress when much against his wishes the cottage was being cleaned up, was no doubt due to his fear of his writings and poetry being burned, rather than to the possible discovery or destruction of hidden five-pound notes. As has been shown by recent research, much of Dicky's writing has been lost, and no doubt a lot of it was destroyed at this time.

The remarks of an elderly gentleman whose memory holds happy visions of his childhood illustrates just what an impression Dicky left upon the minds of his neighbours and his friends. 'To me as a child, Dicky Slader was a familiar figure in my home town of South Molton; even now I can see him, legs dangling, a large basket on one arm, riding into the town on his donkey. I never knew what he carried in the basket, but I do know that he was immediately the centre of attraction, often of ridicule and teasing (shame upon us) of us small boys.'

Mr John Winnifrith, whose grandfather sold Dicky his donkey, writes as one of the younger generation who only came to know about him through his fame.

> My father brought me up on a whole saga of stories about a local family of farmers called Slader. The stories were almost folklore and nearly all centred on the cunning of the youngest child called Richard.
>
> In my youth I was taken by my father to Mariansleigh and we paid a visit to see Richard. He lived alone in a house on a smallholding on the road to Exmoor and was by then a notable eccentric. I remember going up to his bedroom where he kept his stock of ginger beer and feeling less keen about drinking it when I saw how it was kept. The room was a vast collection of ginger beer bottles and chamber pots, both of which he apparently collected.

Within the span of his life Dicky witnessed a great change.

He was born in the early days of the industrial revolution which had still not affected the rural counties of the Westcountry. He died at a time when the motor car and the aeroplane had become commonplace and even the country cottages had running water and electricity. He saw nearly all his relations leave the land, to work in the cities, to serve in the army, or to sail away as emigrants.

The sayings, the hymns and the poetry of Dicky Slader live on beneath the wild moor and across to Barnstaple Bay. Thirty-seven years later his story is recorded. A story worthy, I believe, of preservation.